OFFICIAL SQA PAST PAPERS WITH SQA ANSWERS

Standard Grade Credit FRENCH

1997 to 2001 with two years' answers

© Copyright Scottish Qualifications Authority

First exam paper published in 1997.

Published by
Leckie & Leckie Ltd, 8 Whitehill Terrace, St. Andrews, Scotland KY16 8RN
tel: 01334 475656 fax: 01334 477392
hq@leckieandleckie.co.uk www.leckieandleckie.co.uk

Leckie & Leckie Project Management Team: Tom Davie; David Nicoll; Bruce Ryan, Andrea Smith
Cover Design Assistance: Mike Middleton

ISBN 1-84372-002-7

A CIP Catalogue record for this book is available from the British Library.

Printed in Scotland by Inglis Allen on environmentally friendly paper. The paper is made from a mixture of sawmill waste, forest thinnings and wood from sustainable forests.

® Leckie & Leckie is a registered trademark.

INVESTOR IN PEOPLE Leckie & Leckie Ltd achieved the Investors in People Standard in 1999.

Leckie & Leckie

Introduction

The best way to prepare for exams is to practise, again and again, all that you have learned over the past year. Attempt these questions and check your solutions against these *Official SQA Answers*. But give yourself a real chance and be honest! Doing this will help you gain not only a proper understanding of each topic but also the maximum marks possible from the examiners! Developing this working habit now will make it easier to do this in the exam!

Leckie & Leckie's Standard Grade French Course Notes with Audio Cassette. Learning French is made easier with our superb cassette. This lifts the language off the page, inspiring you to consider other tricky aspects such as spelling and grammar in a different light.

Contents

1997 Exam
Standard Grade French Credit Reading 3
Standard Grade French Credit Listening 11
Standard Grade French Credit Writing 19

1998 Exam
Standard Grade French Credit Reading 23
Standard Grade French Credit Listening 31
Standard Grade French Credit Writing 39

1999 Exam
Standard Grade French Credit Reading 43
Standard Grade French Credit Listening 47
Standard Grade French Credit Writing 55

2000 Exam
Standard Grade French Credit Reading 59
Standard Grade French Credit Listening 67
Standard Grade French Credit Writing 75

2001 Exam
Standard Grade French Credit Reading 79
Standard Grade French Credit Listening 87
Standard Grade French Credit Writing 95

1000/103

SCOTTISH
CERTIFICATE OF
EDUCATION
1997

WEDNESDAY, 21 MAY
1.45 PM – 2.45 PM

FRENCH
STANDARD GRADE
Credit Level
Reading

Instructions to the Candidate

When you are told to do so, open your paper and write your answers **in English** in the **separate** answer book provided.

You may use a French dictionary.

SCOTTISH
QUALIFICATIONS
AUTHORITY

©

THB 1000/103 6/3/24910

1. You are reading a French magazine. You find this article about a young French ski champion.

Laure, la surdouée du ski!

Laure Durand a juste 13 ans. A première vue, rien ne la différencie des autres adolescentes de son âge. Enfin, presque rien . . . Mais, en réalité, Laure est une surdouée du ski.

Laure suit des cours au collège de Briançon (Hautes-Alpes). Entre les heures de mathématiques et de français, elle chausse ses skis et part rejoindre les pistes qu'elle aime tant. Le lundi et le jeudi après-midi, elle skie avec l'école. Le mercredi, le samedi et le dimanche, elle skie avec son club.

Lorsque Laure rate des cours à cause du ski, elle demande à sa meilleure amie de les lui passer. En plus, tous les soirs en semaine, elle est obligée de travailler pour rattraper les cours. Par conséquent, notre championne ne regarde pas la télévision et se couche tôt tous les soirs, même en vacances.

A 13 ans, Laure s'est qualifiée pour la Topolino (une sorte de jeux olympiques pour les jeunes), en Italie, et aux Ménuires, en Savoie, elle a gagné la finale du slalom. Mais ce qu'on a oublié de vous dire, c'est qu'elle a terminé sa course sur un seul ski. Quelques mètres plus haut, elle avait cogné une porte* et avait perdu un ski. Et comme rien ne l'arrête, elle a quand même continué à skier.

«C'est vrai que, pour l'instant, le ski, ça marche plutôt bien pour moi,» reconnaît Laure. «Mais je garde la tête sur les épaules. Quand je rentrerai au lycée, cela sera de plus en plus difficile de suivre des cours et de skier en même temps.»

Mais elle a toujours le sourire aux lèvres . . . Elle sait qu'elle a encore de belles descentes devant elle.

*une porte = a slalom gate

Marks

(a)   What is the first impression we get of Laure?   **(1)**

(b)   (i)   How does Laure keep up with her school work?   **(2)**

        (ii)   How does this affect her routine at home?   **(2)**

(c)   What made her victory at Les Ménuires exceptional?   **(1)**

(d)   (i)   How has she reacted to her success so far?   **(1)**

        (ii)   What difficulty does she see ahead of her?   **(1)**

2. This article is about a dramatic event.

Fusillade à Paris

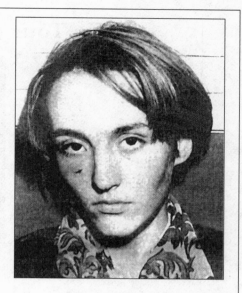

Le 4 octobre, deux policiers et un chauffeur de taxi ont été tués à Paris par Florence Rey (19 ans) et par Marc Maupin (22 ans). Six autres personnes ont été blessées dans les fusillades.

Mardi 4 octobre, 21h 25, un homme et une femme masqués attaquent deux policiers de garde. L'homme et la femme prennent les armes (les revolvers) des policiers. Ils arrêtent un chauffeur de taxi et le prennent en otage avec le passager qu'il transporte.

Quelques minutes après, le chauffeur de taxi voit une voiture de police. Pour attirer l'attention des policiers, il cogne leur voiture. La fusillade éclate. Deux policiers et le chauffeur de taxi sont tués. Marc Maupin est gravement blessé, Florence Rey est arrêtée. Il est 21h 50. En moins d'une heure, trois personnes sont mortes. C'est horrible!

Marc Maupin a 22 ans et est étudiant. Florence Rey a 19 ans. Rien ne laissait penser qu'un jour ils allaient faire un tel crime. Ils n'avaient jamais fait de bêtises avant. Ils n'étaient pas des délinquants. Alors, pourquoi une telle violence?

Ce drame pose beaucoup de questions, et surtout cette question: notre société, est-elle capable de donner aux jeunes autre chose que de la violence? Si aujourd'hui des jeunes tuent pour rien, cela montre que quelque chose ne marche pas bien dans notre société. Cela veut dire qu'ils ne croient plus en rien, que plus rien n'a d'importance pour eux, même pas la vie. Et ça, c'est très grave.

Marks

(*a*) How did the drama begin? **(1)**

(*b*) How did the taxi driver become involved? **(1)**

(*c*) Describe the events which then led to the three deaths. **(3)**

(*d*) Why was the behaviour of these two young people so unexpected? **(2)**

(*e*) What does the author think causes some young people to turn to violence so readily today? **(2)**

3. You then read an article about an unusual journey.

Un Tour du Monde à Vélo en 14 ans

Claude et Françoise Hervé avaient respectivement 27 et 25 ans lorsqu'ils ont transformé leur rêve en réalité: parcourir le monde à vélo.

Le 1er avril 1981, Claude et Françoise ont quitté Lyon sur leurs bicyclettes à quinze vitesses, spécialement construites pour l'occasion et chargées de 70 kilos d'équipement. Après avoir préparé leur voyage pendant deux ans, ils ont renoncé à la sécurité d'un bon job et ont vendu leur appartement de huit pièces.

Le voyage qui devait durer deux ans s'est transformé en une véritable odyssée: ils sont rentrés en France quatorze ans plus tard après une randonnée à vélo fantastique qui s'est étendue aux cinq continents, sur 160 000 kilomètres, avec une licence de mariage signée au Pakistan, une fillette de six ans née en Nouvelle-Zélande et des milliers d'histoires à raconter.

Claude prend la parole:

«Nous avons lutté contre la tempête de neige à moins 30 pour passer un col à 5 000 mètres.

Il nous a fallu une journée entière pour traverser 4 kilomètres de jungle. En Irak, notre tente a été attaquée, au milieu d'un désert, par des chiens sauvages. En Inde, les douaniers de la frontière pakistanaise ont refusé d'accepter mon passeport.

Mais nous ne regrettons pas un instant de nous être lancés dans cette grande aventure.»

Question 3 (continued)

Marks

(a) What did Claude and Françoise have to do before they set off on their journey? Mention **three** things.

(3)

(b) How did their original plans change?

(1)

(c) How had their circumstances changed by the time they returned?

(2)

(d) Describe any **three** things which happened to them during the journey.

(3)

[END OF QUESTION PAPER]

Total (26)

[BLANK PAGE]

[BLANK PAGE]

[BLANK PAGE]

1000/109

SCOTTISH
CERTIFICATE OF
EDUCATION
1997

WEDNESDAY, 21 MAY
3.05 PM – 3.35 PM
(APPROX.)

FRENCH
STANDARD GRADE
Credit Level
Listening Transcript

This paper must not be seen by any candidate.

The material overleaf is provided for use only in an emergency (e.g. the tape or equipment proving faulty) or where arrangements have been agreed in advance for candidates with special needs. The material must be read exactly as printed.

SCOTTISH
QUALIFICATIONS
AUTHORITY

©

Transcript—Credit Level

> **Instructions to reader(s):**
>
> For each item, read the English **once,** then read the French **twice,** with an interval of 7 seconds between the two readings. On completion of the second reading, pause for the length of time indicated in brackets after each item, to allow the candidates to write their answers.
>
> Where special arrangements have been agreed in advance to allow the reading of the material, those sections marked **(f)** should be read by a female speaker and those marked **(m)** by a male: those sections marked **(t)** should be read by the teacher.

(t) You are staying at the home of your French pen pal, Marie-Claire. One day, she talks about how she gets on with her parents.

(m) **Tu loges chez ta correspondante française, Marie-Claire. Un jour, elle te raconte comment**
or   **elle s'entend avec ses parents.**
(f)

(t) **Question number one.**

Marie-Claire sometimes has arguments with her parents.

What do they say? Why does she think this is unfair?

(f) **Je ne m'entends pas du tout avec mes parents. Ils disent que je dépense trop d'argent en vêtements. Pourtant, c'est moi qui travaille pour cet argent, c'est moi qui le gagne. A mon avis, si l'on gagne de l'argent, on a le droit de le dépenser comme on veut.**

(40 seconds)

(t) One evening, Marie-Claire and her father are talking about their summer holiday.

Question number two.

Her father wants to go to Brittany. Why? Give **two** reasons.

(m) **Alors, les vacances! Nous irons en Bretagne, comme d'habitude. J'adore ça. L'air pur de la campagne, la tranquillité et les longues promenades.**

(40 seconds)

(t) **Question number three.**

Why does Marie-Claire not like Brittany? Give **two** reasons.

(f) **La Bretagne, bof! Oh non! Pas encore! On y est allé l'année dernière. Le paysage est joli, mais il n'y a rien à faire. En plus, il ne fait pas chaud.**

(40 seconds)

(t) **Question number four.**

What does she expect from a holiday? Mention **three** things.

(f) **Moi, je veux aller dans un endroit où il y a le soleil et la mer bleue; et où je peux sortir le soir avec d'autres jeunes. Pourquoi ne pas aller en Italie ou en Espagne?**

(40 seconds)

(t) Question number five.

Why can they not afford to go abroad?

(m) Ah, non! Tu sais très bien qu'on ne peut pas se payer un voyage à l'étranger cette année. Cela nous coûtera assez cher quand tu vas partir aux Etats-Unis avec ton école!

(40 seconds)

(t) Question number six.

Her father suggests going to Nice. How will they be able to afford this?

(m) Si tu veux du soleil, j'ai un collègue de bureau qui a un appartement près de Nice. Je crois qu'on pourra y loger gratuitement.

(40 seconds)

(t) Question number seven.

Her father wants to take the train this year. Why? Mention **one** thing.

(m) De toute façon, on va prendre le train cette année. Il y a trop de circulation sur les routes. J'en ai assez des embouteillages quand on part en vacances.

(40 seconds)

(t) Question number eight.

Her father gives **two** more reasons for not travelling by car. What are they?

(m) D'ailleurs, les routes sont dangereuses à cette saison. Chaque année, au moment des grands départs, des centaines de personnes sont tuées ou blessées.

(40 seconds)

(t) Question number nine.

Marie-Claire tells you about her favourite holiday.

What made it so enjoyable for her? Mention any **two** things.

(f) Ma meilleure expérience de vacances en groupe, c'était quand j'avais douze ans. Je suis partie dans les Pyrénées avec un groupe de cent enfants de neuf nationalités pour une semaine d'activités en plein air—des cours de canoë, des cours d'escalade, des choses comme ça.

(40 seconds)

(t) One day, you go to school with Marie-Claire. During one class, a doctor comes in to talk to pupils about young people's eating habits.

Question number ten.

What does the doctor say about young people's breakfast habits? Why does she advise against this?

(f) Beaucoup de jeunes quittent la maison le matin sans rien manger. Ce n'est pas une bonne idée parce qu'ils n'ont pas assez d'énergie pour travailler jusqu'à midi.

(40 seconds)

[Turn over for Questions 11 to 13 on *Page four*

(t) Question number eleven.

What sort of breakfast does the doctor recommend? What advice does she give about mid-morning snacks?
Mention **one** thing.

(f) Il faut manger équilibré. Le matin, prenez des céréales avec du lait chaud et une boisson
chaude. Si vous avez faim à dix heures, évitez les produits sucrés. A la place, mangez un
fruit, qui vous donne des vitamines.

(40 seconds)

(t) Question number twelve.

What have many young people stopped doing at lunchtime? What does the doctor say about eating "fast
food"? Mention **one** thing.

(f) A midi, de plus en plus de jeunes abandonnent les cantines des collèges pour aller dans les
"fast-foods". Manger dans un "fast-food" de temps en temps ne fait pas de mal—mais pas
tous les jours.

(40 seconds)

(t) Question number thirteen.

What is her biggest concern about this type of food? Mention **one** thing.

(f) Les hamburgers et les frites contiennent trop de graisse. Si on ne change pas ces
habitudes, à l'avenir on aura beaucoup de gens avec des problèmes de santé très sérieux.

(40 seconds)

(t) End of test.

You now have 5 minutes to look over your answers.

[END OF TRANSCRIPT]

1000/108

SCOTTISH
CERTIFICATE OF
EDUCATION
1997

WEDNESDAY, 21 MAY
3.05 PM – 3.35 PM
(APPROX.)

FRENCH
STANDARD GRADE
Credit Level

Listening

Instructions to the Candidate

When you are told to do so, open your paper.

You will hear a number of short items in French. You will hear each item twice, then you will have time to write your answer.

Write your answers, **in English**, in the **separate** answer book provided.

You may take notes as you are listening to the French, but only in your answer book.

You may **not** use a French dictionary.

You are not allowed to leave the examination room until the end of the test.

SCOTTISH
QUALIFICATIONS
AUTHORITY

©

THB 1000/108 6/3/24910

Marks

You are staying at the home of your French pen pal, Marie-Claire. One day, she talks about how she gets on with her parents.

Tu loges chez ta correspondante française, Marie-Claire. Un jour, elle te raconte comment elle s'entend avec ses parents.

1. Marie-Claire sometimes has arguments with her parents.

    (*a*) What do they say?   **(1)**

    (*b*) Why does she think this is unfair?   **(2)**

                    *   *   *   *   *

One evening, Marie-Claire and her father are talking about their summer holiday.

2. Her father wants to go to Brittany. Why? Give **two** reasons.   **(2)**

                    *   *   *   *   *

3. Why does Marie-Claire not like Brittany? Give **two** reasons.   **(2)**

                    *   *   *   *   *

4. What does she expect from a holiday? Mention **three** things.   **(3)**

                    *   *   *   *   *

5. Why can they not afford to go abroad?   **(1)**

                    *   *   *   *   *

6. Her father suggests going to Nice. How will they be able to afford this? **(1)**

                    *   *   *   *   *

7. Her father wants to take the train this year. Why? Mention **one** thing. **(1)**

                    *   *   *   *   *

8. Her father gives **two** more reasons for not travelling by car. What are they? **(2)**

                    *   *   *   *   *

9. Marie-Claire tells you about her favourite holiday.

    What made it so enjoyable for her? Mention any **two** things.   **(2)**

                    *   *   *   *   *

Marks

One day, you go to school with Marie-Claire. During one class, a doctor comes in to talk to pupils about young people's eating habits.

10. (a) What does the doctor say about young people's breakfast habits?   **(1)**

    (b) Why does she advise against this?   **(1)**

*   *   *   *   *

11. (a) What sort of breakfast does the doctor recommend?   **(2)**

    (b) What advice does she give about mid-morning snacks? Mention **one** thing.   **(1)**

*   *   *   *   *

12. (a) What have many young people stopped doing at lunchtime?   **(1)**

    (b) What does the doctor say about eating "fast food"? Mention **one** thing.   **(1)**

*   *   *   *   *

13. What is her biggest concern about this type of food? Mention **one** thing.   **(1)**

*   *   *   *   *

Total (25)

[END OF QUESTION PAPER]

[BLANK PAGE]

C

1001/111

SCOTTISH
CERTIFICATE OF
EDUCATION
1997
THURSDAY, 22 MAY
2.05 PM – 3.05 PM

FRENCH
STANDARD GRADE
Credit Level
(Optional Paper)
Writing

SCOTTISH
QUALIFICATIONS
AUTHORITY

©

Some young French people have written to a magazine with their views on holidays.

"J'aime bien partir à l'étranger car ça permet de découvrir une autre culture et des gens différents. En particulier, j'adore voyager en Europe. Et aujourd'hui, ce n'est pas cher de voyager en Europe."

Bernard, 16 ans

"Moi, j'aime passer mes vacances dans les pays chauds car j'aime le soleil. J'adore me faire bronzer et aller à la plage. C'est agréable de se promener le soir sans avoir à porter un pullover."

Laure, 15 ans

"J'ai fait un très bon voyage scolaire quand j'avais 13 ans. J'ai passé une semaine à la montagne avec ma classe. Dans la journée nous faisions du ski, et le soir, des jeux."

Georges, 14 ans

"Moi, de toute façon, je préfère partir en vacances avec mes copains. C'est vrai, avec mes parents, je ne peux jamais faire ce que je veux. Avec mes copains, je sors en boîte et je me couche à l'heure qui me plaît."

Nicole, 16 ans

"Quand je quitterai le collège, j'aimerais attendre un an avant de chercher un emploi. J'ai l'intention de mettre toutes mes affaires dans un sac à dos et de prendre la route pour voyager en Afrique."

François, 15 ans

Now that you have read these people's thoughts on holidays, write about your own views.

Here are some questions you may wish to consider. You do not have to use all of them, and you are free to include other relevant ideas.

- Do you generally go away on holiday?
- Do you prefer holidays with your family or with friends?
- What do you think of school trips?
- What sort of holiday do you prefer?
- Have you had any particularly memorable holidays?
- What are your plans for this summer?
- Where would you most like to go on holiday and why?

Write about 200 words in **French**.

You may use a French dictionary.

[END OF QUESTION PAPER]

[BLANK PAGE]

C

1000/103

SCOTTISH
CERTIFICATE OF
EDUCATION
1998

TUESDAY, 19 MAY
10.15 AM – 11.15 AM

FRENCH
STANDARD GRADE
Credit Level
Reading

Instructions to the Candidate

When you are told to do so, open your paper and write your answers **in English** in the **separate** answer book provided.

You may use a French dictionary.

Marks

1. In a French magazine, you read this article about security in French cities.

Sécurité renforcée dans les villes françaises

L'année dernière, on a vu plusieurs attentats terroristes dans les villes françaises—notamment la bombe qui a explosé au mois d'octobre à la sortie d'une station de métro à Paris et qui a fait deux morts. En plus, les incidents violents sont en hausse à l'intérieur des écoles.

Donc, le gouvernement a lancé le Plan Vigipirate. Il est interdit de stationner devant les bâtiments publics—par exemple, les gares, les stations de métro, les mairies, les écoles et les lycées. L'entrée de toute personne étrangère dans les mairies et les écoles est strictement contrôlée.

(a) Why is there a need for increased security in French cities?   **(1)**

(b) Give details of the incident which happened last October.   **(2)**

(c) What has the "Plan Vigipirate" done to help things?   **(2)**

Marks

2.   The article continues.

┌───┐
│   │
│   ┌───┐   │
│   │   . . . et dans les établissements scolaires   │   │
│   └───┘   │
│   │
│   Quant à la sécurité à l'intérieur des écoles, le ministre de l'Éducation │
│   Nationale a pris plusieurs mesures: │
│   │
│   • Le jour de la rentrée, les enseignants liront le règlement intérieur et en │
│   discuteront avec leurs élèves. Comme ça, tous les lycéens comprendront │
│   ce qui est permis et ce qui ne l'est pas.   │
│   │
│   • Dans les collèges et les lycées, l'autorité des professeurs est renforcée │
│   avec la possibilité d'interrompre un cours lorsqu'il y a un problème de │
│   violence. Cela permettra la discussion entre professeurs et élèves. │
│   │
│   • Les nouveaux enseignants recevront une formation spéciale pour leur │
│   apprendre à trouver la meilleure solution face à une situation de │
│   violence (comme les bagarres).   │
│   │
│   • De plus, cette année, 5 000 appelés (des jeunes qui font leur service │
│   militaire) se retrouveront dans les collèges et les lycées. Leur travail │
│   sera d'éviter les bagarres entre élèves en discutant et en écoutant petits │
│   et grands.   │
│   │
└───┘

(a)   In schools, what will happen on the first day of term?   **(1)**

(b)   What will be done to help new teachers?   **(1)**

(c)   How are people doing military service going to help?   **(2)**

[Turn over

Marks

3. You read this article which gives you tips on how to organise your schoolwork.

COMMENT VOUS ORGANISER POUR L'ANNÉE SCOLAIRE

Au début de l'année scolaire, tu t'es promis de bien travailler. Mais c'est plus facile à dire qu'à faire. Voici quelques idées pour t'aider.

- **Du plus facile au plus difficile**

  Le plus dur, c'est de commencer à travailler. Il vaut mieux démarrer par un exercice que tu aimes bien ou une leçon que tu trouves facile. Ensuite, tu pourras faire les devoirs plus difficiles.

- **La bonne dose**

  Dès que tu rentres à la maison, mets-toi au travail tout de suite! Plonge-toi dans tes devoirs pendant quelque temps. Ensuite, accorde-toi une demi-heure de détente; prends un bain ou regarde la télévision ou téléphone à un copain. Puis, reprends ton travail.

- **Fixe-toi des objectifs!**

  Inutile de prendre de grandes résolutions que tu ne pourras pas tenir. Mieux vaut te fixer de petits objectifs, jour après jour, semaine après semaine. Par exemple, décide de travailler régulièrement tous les jours et d'augmenter tes notes petit à petit; n'essaie pas d'être le premier de la classe!

- **. . . et le bilan?**

  Si tu travailles bien et obtiens de bonnes notes, tu pourras négocier avec tes parents quand tu voudras regarder un film à la télévision ou sortir avec tes copains.

(a) It is hard to get down to work. How can you make it easier? **(1)**

(b) How should you organise your evening? **(3)**

(c) What are you told about setting targets for yourself? **(2)**

(d) What benefits could there be for you if you get good marks? **(2)**

4. This article is about a highly successful French woman cyclist, known as "La Petite Reine".

> ### La "Petite Reine" Jeannie Longo
> ### Le plus beau palmarès du sport français
>
> 32 fois championne de France, 10 fois championne du monde, médaillée d'or et d'argent aux Jeux d'Atlanta. Comment fait Jeannie Longo pour tout gagner? Elle est la plus douée et la plus travailleuse des cyclistes. À chaque concours, elle participe aux deux épreuves qui existent sur route: la course "en ligne" et le "contre-la-montre". Sur piste, elle détient aussi le record du monde de vitesse.
>
> #### En ligne ou contre-la-montre?
>
> Dans la course "en ligne", toutes les concurrentes partent ensemble. Aux Jeux Olympiques, Jeannie a franchi la ligne d'arrivée en tête. Dans le "contre-la-montre", elles partent les unes après les autres, toutes les 2 minutes pour ne pas se gêner. À l'arrivée, on calcule les temps. À Atlanta, une jeune Russe de 23 ans a été plus rapide que la Française. Médaille d'or pour elle, d'argent pour Jeannie.
>
> #### "Mes poules et mes légumes"
>
> Le secret de Jeannie, c'est peut-être ce qu'elle mange. Dans son chalet près de Grenoble, elle élève trois poules pondeuses (Cachou, Frétille et Négrita). Dans son jardin elle cultive des haricots, des artichauts et des betteraves entre d'autres. "Tout le monde se moque de mon alimentation, mais elle est très saine, car je peux manger les œufs de mes poules et je fais des soupes avec mes légumes.
>
> #### "Mon entraînement"
>
> Mais le régime ne fait pas tout, il faut d'abord s'entraîner. Jeannie parcourt toute l'année, même l'hiver, des milliers de kilomètres, parfois en VTT*. Elle travaille aussi chez elle: "Je travaille beaucoup ma puissance en faisant de l'haltérophilie. L'hiver dernier, j'ai pris deux bons kilos de muscles . . . "

*vélo tout-terrain

Marks

(a) Give details of Jeannie Longo's success at the Atlanta Olympic games. **(1)**

(b) Why is she such a successful cyclist? **(2)**

(c) Explain the differences between the "En ligne" and "Contre-la-montre" road races. **(2)**

(d) How does she make sure that the food she eats is healthy? **(2)**

(e) What does she do to stay in peak condition? **(2)**

Total (26)

[END OF QUESTION PAPER]

[BLANK PAGE]

[BLANK PAGE]

[BLANK PAGE]

C

1000/109

SCOTTISH
CERTIFICATE OF
EDUCATION
1998

TUESDAY, 19 MAY
1.00 PM – 1.30 PM
(APPROX.)

FRENCH
STANDARD GRADE
Credit Level
Listening Transcript

This paper must not be seen by any candidate.

The material overleaf is provided for use in an emergency only (eg the tape or equipment proving faulty) or where permission has been given in advance by the SQA for the material to be read to candidates with special needs. The material must be read exactly as printed.

SCOTTISH
QUALIFICATIONS
AUTHORITY

Transcript—Credit Level

Instructions to reader(s):

For each item, read the English **once,** then read the French **twice,** with an interval of 7 seconds between the two readings. On completion of the second reading, pause for the length of time indicated in brackets after each item, to allow the candidates to write their answers.

Where special arrangements have been agreed in advance to allow the reading of the material, those sections marked **(f)** should be read by a female speaker and those marked **(m)** by a male: those sections marked **(t)** should be read by the teacher.

(t)   You are staying with your French pen pal, Marianne, who lives near Paris.

Marianne is talking to her father about going into the city centre to show you the famous monuments.

(f)   **Vous passez des vacances chez votre correspondante française, Marianne, qui habite près**
or   **de Paris.**
(m)

Marianne et son père parlent de visiter les monuments au centre de Paris.

(t)   Question number one.

According to Marianne's father, what is the difficulty about driving in Paris? What example of this does he give?

(m)   **Il est difficile de rouler à Paris maintenant. Tu sais, il y a tant de voitures. Quelquefois, en rentrant du bureau, il me faut une heure pour faire un kilomètre.**

(40 seconds)

(t)   Question number two.

Why are things a little easier in August? What is often the problem at that time of year?

(m)   **Mais, au mois d'août, tous les Parisiens partent en vacances, et il y a de la place sur les routes. Le seul inconvénient, c'est qu'il fait souvent très chaud entre midi et trois heures. Par conséquent, il est impossible de sortir en voiture.**

(40 seconds)

(t)   Question number three.

Marianne's father suggests that you take the train to the centre of Paris.

In his opinion, what are the advantages of travelling in this way? Mention **three** things.

(m)   **Ce n'est pas la peine de prendre la voiture. Avec le train, nous arriverons au centre de Paris dans vingt minutes. Puis, nous pourrons prendre le Métro pour visiter les monuments. Comme ça, pas besoin de chercher un parking.**

(40 seconds)

(t) Question number four.

Why does Marianne think the Métro is dangerous? What happened to her friend, Anne-Louise, last year?

(f)   Oui, Papa, mais le Métro est dangereux! Il y a parfois des actes de terrorisme dans les stations. Et puis, l'année dernière, on a volé un sac à ma copine, Anne-Louise.

(40 seconds)

(t) Question number five.

What advice does Marianne's father give about travelling safely by Métro?

(m)   C'est vrai qu'il peut être dangereux. Mais les actes de terrorisme sont rares. Il n'y a pas de problème si on ne voyage pas entre quatre heures et six heures de l'après-midi, et si on est accompagné. La plupart des victimes de vols voyagent seules.

(40 seconds)

(t) Question number six.

One evening you are listening to the radio. A young star of French cinema is being interviewed.

What did she do from the age of 8? What happened when she was fifteen? Why?

(f)   J'ai toujours voulu être actrice, même quand j'étais toute petite. A l'âge de 8 ans déjà, je jouais régulièrement dans des pièces de théâtre à l'école. A l'âge de 15 ans, mes parents ont décidé de déménager à Paris pour me donner toutes les chances de réussir.

(40 seconds)

(t) Question number seven.

She continues.

What made it difficult to break into the profession? What sort of work did she finally get?

(f)   Au début, j'ai eu beaucoup de difficultés à trouver du travail. Il y a énormément de jeunes qui voudraient entrer dans cette profession et très peu de rôles pour les personnes de mon âge. Heureusement, après quelques mois, j'ai obtenu de petits rôles dans des séries télévisées.

(40 seconds)

(t) Question number eight.

She talks about how she was picked to be the star in a French film about a young ballet dancer.

Explain what was involved in the selection process. Why was she chosen?

(f)   J'ai d'abord participé à un casting de 500 filles. Ensuite, on a choisi dix d'entre nous pour rencontrer le producteur. Finalement, j'ai réussi à être sélectionnée parce que j'étais la plus athlétique et donc la plus capable d'apprendre la danse classique.

(40 seconds)

[Turn over for Questions 9 and 10 on *Page four*

(t) Question number nine.

What does she say about her private life? Mention any **two** things.

(f)   **Mon succès n'a rien changé. Je connais mon petit ami depuis deux ans et mes copines sont toujours les mêmes.**

(40 seconds)

(t) Question number ten.

What does she tell us about her situation at the moment?

(f)   **J'ai terminé l'école et je désire rester dans le cinéma, même si c'est quelquefois difficile. Pour le moment, l'argent n'est pas un problème, donc je ne dois pas chercher mon prochain rôle immédiatement.**

(40 seconds)

(t) End of test.

You now have 5 minutes to look over your answers.

[*END OF TRANSCRIPT*]

1000/108

SCOTTISH
CERTIFICATE OF
EDUCATION
1998

TUESDAY, 19 MAY
1.00 PM – 1.30 PM
(APPROX.)

FRENCH
STANDARD GRADE
Credit Level
Listening

Instructions to the Candidate

When you are told to do so, open your paper.

You will hear a number of short items in French. You will hear each item twice, then you will have time to write your answer.

Write your answers, **in English**, in the **separate** answer book provided.

You may take notes as you are listening to the French, but only in your answer book.

You may **not** use a French dictionary.

You are not allowed to leave the examination room until the end of the test.

SCOTTISH
QUALIFICATIONS
AUTHORITY

Marks

You are staying with your French pen pal, Marianne, who lives near Paris.

Marianne is talking to her father about going into the city centre to show you the famous monuments.

Vous passez des vacances chez votre correspondante française, Marianne, qui habite près de Paris.

Marianne et son père parlent de visiter les monuments au centre de Paris.

1. (a) According to Marianne's father, what is the difficulty about driving in Paris?   **(1)**

    (b) What example of this does he give?   **(1)**

*   *   *   *   *

2. (a) Why are things a little easier in August?   **(1)**

    (b) What is often the problem at that time of year?   **(1)**

*   *   *   *   *

3. Marianne's father suggests that you take the train to the centre of Paris.

    In his opinion, what are the advantages of travelling in this way? Mention **three** things.   **(3)**

*   *   *   *   *

4. (a) Why does Marianne think the Métro is dangerous?   **(1)**

    (b) What happened to her friend, Anne-Louise, last year?   **(1)**

*   *   *   *   *

5. What advice does Marianne's father give about travelling safely by Métro?   **(2)**

*   *   *   *   *

6. One evening you are listening to the radio. A young star of French cinema is being interviewed.

    (a) What did she do from the age of 8?   **(1)**

    (b) What happened when she was fifteen? Why?   **(2)**

*   *   *   *   *

7. She continues.

    (a) What made it difficult to break into the profession?   **(2)**

    (b) What sort of work did she finally get?   **(1)**

*   *   *   *   *

Marks

8. She talks about how she was picked to be the star in a French film about a young ballet dancer.

   (*a*) Explain what was involved in the selection process. **(2)**

   (*b*) Why was she chosen? **(1)**

   *   *   *   *   *

9. What does she say about her private life? Mention any **two** things. **(2)**

   *   *   *   *   *

10. What does she tell us about her situation at the moment? **(3)**

   *   *   *   *   *

   Total (25)

[END OF QUESTION PAPER]

[BLANK PAGE]

1001/111

SCOTTISH
CERTIFICATE OF
EDUCATION
1998

TUESDAY, 19 MAY
2.50 PM – 3.50 PM

FRENCH
STANDARD GRADE
Credit Level
(Optional Paper)
Writing

Several French teenagers comment about their home area.

J'habite dans une ville au centre de la France. Il y a deux cinémas, pas mal de jardins publics, un grand centre sportif, et aussi beaucoup de magasins. Que demander de plus?

Marcel, 15 ans

Je ne supporte pas de vivre dans un appartement. Mon quartier est bien trop bruyant et animé, l'atmosphère est polluée et les gens sont tout le temps pressés et stressés.

Nadine, 15 ans

Mes parents ont décidé d'habiter à la campagne. Mais je vais au collège dans la ville d'à côté. Après l'école, je dois prendre le bus au lieu de rester avec mes copains. Le week-end, je ne peux pas sortir souvent. C'est pas la joie!

Jérôme, 16 ans

J'ai déménagé à Paris il y a cinq ans. Avant, j'habitais dans une petite ville. Je n'arrive pas à m'habituer à Paris. Je n'ai pas beaucoup d'amis. Mes parents ne me laissent pas sortir seule. Ils pensent que c'est trop dangereux. C'est pénible!

Claire, 16 ans

J'aimerais bien habiter en ville. J'apprécie l'anonymat qu'offre une grande ville. Il y a aussi beaucoup de choses à faire et à voir dans une ville: cinémas, musées, expos, théâtres, opéras, concerts. On peut sans cesse découvrir de nouveaux endroits.

Félix, 15 ans

Now that you have read these people's thoughts on where they live, give your own opinions about where you live.

Here are some questions you may wish to consider. You do not have to use all of them, and you are free to include other relevant ideas.

- Where do you live?

- What is your town/village/area like?

- What do you like/dislike about where you live?

- What is there to do?

- How do you spend your time there?

- Have you ever lived anywhere else?

- Where would you most like to live?

Write about 200 words in **French**.

You may use a French dictionary.

[END OF QUESTION PAPER]

[BLANK PAGE]

1000/103

SCOTTISH
CERTIFICATE OF
EDUCATION
1999

TUESDAY, 18 MAY
10.25 AM – 11.25 AM

FRENCH
STANDARD GRADE
Credit Level
Reading

Instructions to the Candidate

When you are told to do so, open your paper and write your answers **in English** in the **separate** answer book provided.

You may use a French dictionary.

SCOTTISH
QUALIFICATIONS
AUTHORITY

Marks

Your French pen friend has sent you a magazine.

1.   You read this article about poverty.

Lutter contre la Pauvreté

Où sont les pays pauvres?

Partout dans le monde, il y a des pays pauvres. Par exemple, la république d'Haïti, le Mali en Afrique, ou le Bengladesh en Asie. Sur Terre, une personne sur cinq n'a pas d'eau potable à boire. Un être humain sur huit ne mange pas suffisamment et ne peut pas être soigné quand il est malade. Et un enfant sur trois ne peut pas aller à l'école.

Y a-t-il des pauvres en France?

Même dans les pays riches, comme la France, il y a des pauvres. Un français sur vingt vit dans une grande pauvreté. Et certains enfants de France n'ont qu'un seul repas par jour: celui de la cantine. Ces enfants manquent de vitamines et ils attrapent des maladies.

Qui sont les pauvres, comment les aider?

«Ils passent leur journée dans le métro. On les appelle les SDF (sans domicile fixe). C'est pas génial. Alors on pourrait leur envoyer des sous ou des médicaments.»

Laurence, 9 ans

«Ce sont les gens qui sont au chômage, c'est-à-dire sans boulot. C'est pas juste. Ils manquent d'amitié, alors on devrait leur parler, essayer de les comprendre.»

Charles, 9 ans

(*a*)   The first part of the article gives examples of poverty throughout the world. Give details of **two** of these examples.   **(2)**

(*b*)   A number of children in France also live in poverty.

   (i)   What example is given of this?   **(1)**

   (ii) How does this affect their health?   **(2)**

(*c*)   **Who** are the poor and **how** can they be helped

   (i)   according to Laurence?   **(2)**

   (ii) according to Charles?   **(2)**

Marks

2. This article is about a young man who is training to be an acrobatic horse-rider.

Schantih

Schantih vient d'avoir dix-huit ans. Son prénom est indien et signifie "paix", mais, né à Paris, son père est hollandais et sa mère est française. Il travaille avec la fameuse troupe de cirque équestre, le Zingaro. Ainsi, il réalise son grand rêve—vivre avec les chevaux.

Sa passion pour les chevaux a commencé lorsque sa mère, qui est professeur de danse, a décidé de créer un spectacle avec danseurs et chevaux. Shantih a rencontré Joss—voltigeur* dans le spectacle. Joss lui a appris comment faire de la voltige à cheval et désormais Schantih avait une idée fixe: rentrer à l'école de cirque de Châlons-sur-Marne pour devenir voltigeur à cheval.

L'école de Cirque de Châlons est très réputée: elle dure quatre ans. Les deux premières années, on y apprend les techniques de base du cirque comme par exemple la danse, l'acrobatie ou le jonglage. Les deux années suivantes, les élèves choisissent la discipline qui leur plaît. Schantih avait opté pour la voltige à cheval et grâce à son ami, Joss, qui travaille avec cette troupe depuis plusieurs années, il peut effectuer ses deux années de spécialisation au Zingaro.

Schantih est le plus jeune voltigeur du Zingaro. Il travaille chaque numéro pendant des mois. Tout est calculé au millimètre. On le voit debout en équilibre parfait sur son cheval, les bras ouverts vers le public. Jamais il ne glisse ou tombe.

Mais ce n'est pas du cirque. Ici, pas de dompteur . . . Les chevaux sont rois. Eux aussi, ce sont des acteurs avec leur propre personnalité. Ceux qui connaissent les chevaux savent que la complicité entre l'homme et le cheval doit être parfaite pour obtenir un bon travail.

*un voltigeur—an acrobat on horseback

(a) How did Schantih's love of horses begin? **(1)**

(b) He decided to become an acrobat on horseback. What rôle did Joss play in this? **(1)**

(c) How are the four years at the École de Cirque divided up? **(2)**

(d) Why was Joss able to get Schantih a placement with the Zingaro? **(1)**

(e) What makes Schantih such a good performer? **(2)**

(f) What quality do these particular horses have? **(1)**

Marks

3.   You then read about why professional footballers are doing modelling.

Footballeurs modèles

De plus en plus, on voit de jeunes footballeurs célèbres défiler pour les maisons de haute couture françaises et italiennes. Pourquoi?—La raison est très simple: Le sport, et particulièrement le football, tend à devenir un vrai phénomène de société qui touche toutes les classes sociales. Le joueur de foot est le prototype de l'athlète moderne: musclé, élancé et puissant. Les couturiers ont bien reçu ce message et savent profiter du succès de ce sport pour avancer leurs maisons de haute couture.

Et les footballeurs, pourquoi acceptent-ils ces invitations?

Ibou Ba, qui a défilé pour le couturier italien Francesco Smalto, explique: "L'occasion s'est présentée, j'y ai réfléchi et j'ai accepté rapidement. C'est une expérience, un truc à vivre. Ce qui me plaît, c'est d'être le centre du monde. Je trouve l'ambiance dans la salle—les lumières, l'éclat . . . et la flatterie, bien sûr . . . sensationnelle."

Pour Bernard Lama, il est question de s'amuser et de rendre service à la fois. Donc, il a répondu favorablement à l'invitation de Junko Koshino, une créatrice japonaise. Elle déclare: "J'ai rencontré Bernard et je lui ai demandé de défiler pour moi. Son allure, son côté félin m'intéressaient. D'abord, il a ri. Il m'a expliqué qu'il était footballeur et non pas mannequin. Heureusement, j'ai réussi à le convaincre."

Cependant, il y a des exceptions. Habib Sissokho était mannequin avant de devenir footballeur professionnel. "Je jouais à Créteil. Je me baladais aux Champs-Elysées lorsqu'un homme assis à la terrasse d'un café m'a parlé. Je ne le connaissais pas, c'était Paco Rabanne, le célèbre couturier . Il m'a demandé de défiler pour lui et j'ai accepté. J'ai fait pas mal de défilés et bien gagné ma vie, mais à un moment, il a fallu choisir entre la mode et le foot. Je n'ai pas hésité longtemps."

(a)   Why do fashion houses invite footballers to model for them? Mention any **two** things.   **(2)**

(b)   What does Ibou Ba find exciting about modelling? Mention **two** things.   **(2)**

(c)   What does Bernard Lama get out of modelling?   **(1)**

(d)   How did he first react when Junko Koshino asked him to model for her?   **(2)**

(e)   Habib Sissokho was a model before he became a famous footballer. How did he get his lucky break into modelling?   **(2)**

Total (26)

[END OF QUESTION PAPER]

C

1000/109

SCOTTISH
CERTIFICATE OF
EDUCATION
1999

TUESDAY, 18 MAY
1.30 PM – 2.00 PM
(APPROX.)

FRENCH
STANDARD GRADE
Credit Level
Listening Transcript

This paper must not be seen by any candidate.

SCOTTISH
QUALIFICATIONS
AUTHORITY

SQA 1000/109 6/1310

Transcript—Credit Level

> **Instructions to reader(s):**
>
> For each item, read the English **once,** then read the French **twice**, with an interval of 7 seconds between the two readings. On completion of the second reading, pause for the length of time indicated in brackets after each item, to allow the candidates to write their answers.
>
> Where special arrangements have been agreed in advance to allow the reading of the material, those sections marked **(f)** should be read by a female speaker and those marked **(m)** by a male: those sections marked **(t)** should be read by the teacher.

(t) A French assistant visits your class to talk about her experiences during her year in Scotland.

(f)
or
(m)   **Une assistante française vient dans ta classe pour raconter ses expériences pendant son année en Ecosse.**

(t) Question number one.

Your teacher asks her why she has come to Scotland.

Why did she come to Scotland? Give **two** reasons.

(f)   **Je suis venue en Ecosse pour faire des progrès en anglais, et je voulais connaître la culture écossaise.**

(*40 seconds*)

(t) Question number two.

She is asked about her first impressions.

What impressed her most when she arrived? Mention **one** thing. What did she find difficult to start with?

(f)   **J'ai d'abord été impressionnée par les paysages magnifiques et j'ai trouvé les gens vraiment sympa. Mais les premières semaines c'était très difficile de comprendre les élèves.**

(*40 seconds*)

(t) Question number three.

She tells you how she found somewhere to stay.

What steps did she take to find her accommodation? Mention **three** things.

(f)   **J'ai mis des petites annonces dans les journaux et j'ai regardé les annonces affichées dans les magasins. Ensuite, j'ai visité beaucoup d'appartements partout dans la ville.**

(*40 seconds*)

(t) Question number four.

She talks about the flat she has found.

What does she say? Mention any **three** things. How much rent does she pay?

(f)   Finalement, j'ai réussi à trouver un appartement que je partage avec une co-locataire qui est professeur. L'appartement se trouve dans le vieux quartier de la ville. J'ai une chambre à moi et je me sens à l'aise dans l'appartement. Le loyer est de 45 livres par semaine. C'est cher mais tout est compris.

(40 seconds)

(t) Question number five.

She is asked about her flat mate.

Why do they not spend much time together? Mention any **three** things.

(f)   Nous nous voyons peu. Nous sommes toutes les deux très occupées et nous n'avons ni les mêmes passe-temps ni les mêmes habitudes. Je suis rarement là sauf le week-end pendant la journée. Mais parfois nous allons au cinéma ensemble et nous nous entendons assez bien. Il n'y a jamais de dispute entre nous.

(40 seconds)

(t) Question number six.

She explains what she does in her leisure time.

How does she spend her time? Mention any **two** things.

(f)   Deux fois par semaine, je donne des cours particuliers en français. Quelquefois, je vais au pub avec des amis, et j'apprends les danses folkloriques écossaises. Le week-end, j'aime aussi faire des randonnées en montagne.

(40 seconds)

(t) Question number seven.

She talks about her experiences in school.

What comments does she make about Scottish pupils? Mention any **two** things.

(f)   Selon moi, la plupart des élèves sont assez sages en classe. En plus, ils font beaucoup d'efforts pour apprendre le français. Mais j'ai aussi remarqué qu'ils n'ont pas l'habitude de se concentrer sur une matière pendant une heure entière, c'est-à-dire toute la leçon.

(40 seconds)

(t) Question number eight.

She compares schools in France with schools in Scotland.

Why does she prefer the Scottish school system? Mention any **three** things.

(f)   Je préfère le système écossais parce que les journées sont moins longues. En France, on commence à 8h. et on finit à 5h, en général. Je trouve que l'école en France est quelquefois très dure. En Ecosse, les profs sont plus attentifs, plus prêts à aider les élèves en difficulté. Et les élèves ont plus de choix dans leurs études.

(40 seconds)

[Turn over for Questions 9 and 10 on *Page four*

(t) Question number nine.

She is asked if she misses France.

Why does she miss French meal times? Mention **two** things.

(f)   La France ne me manque pas particulièrement, mais je trouve la nourriture écossaise vraiment affreuse. Il y a une grande différence entre les repas français et écossais. En France, nous prenons le temps de bien manger parce que c'est bon pour la digestion.

(40 seconds)

(t) Question number ten.

She tells us what she will do next.

What does she plan to do when she returns to France?

What does she consider to be important in life? Mention **one** thing.

(f)   Après mon année en Ecosse, je rentrerai en France pour continuer mes études. Ce qui est important pour moi dans la vie, c'est d'avoir un travail stable mais aussi d'être heureuse.

(40 seconds)

(t) End of test.

You now have 5 minutes to look over your answers.

[END OF TRANSCRIPT]

C

1000/108

SCOTTISH
CERTIFICATE OF
EDUCATION
1999

TUESDAY, 18 MAY
1.30 PM – 2.00 PM
(APPROX.)

FRENCH
STANDARD GRADE
Credit Level
Listening

Instructions to the Candidate

When you are told to do so, open your paper.

You will hear a number of short items in French. You will hear each item twice, then you will have time to write your answer.

Write your answers, **in English**, in the **separate** answer book provided.

You may take notes as you are listening to the French, but only in your answer book.

You may **not** use a French dictionary.

You are not allowed to leave the examination room until the end of the test.

SCOTTISH
QUALIFICATIONS
AUTHORITY

THB 1000/108 6/24820   ©

Marks

A French assistant visits your class to talk about her experiences during her year in Scotland.

Une assistante française vient dans ta classe pour raconter ses expériences pendant son année en Ecosse.

1. Your teacher asks her why she has come to Scotland.

Why did she come to Scotland? Give **two** reasons.   **(2)**

*   *   *   *   *

2. She is asked about her first impressions.

(*a*) What impressed her most when she arrived? Mention **one** thing.   **(1)**

(*b*) What did she find difficult to start with?   **(1)**

*   *   *   *   *

3. She tells you how she found somewhere to stay.

What steps did she take to find her accommodation? Mention **three** things.   **(3)**

*   *   *   *   *

4. She talks about the flat she has found.

(*a*) What does she say? Mention any **three** things.   **(3)**

(*b*) How much rent does she pay?   **(1)**

*   *   *   *   *

5. She is asked about her flat mate.

Why do they not spend much time together? Mention any **three** things.   **(3)**

*   *   *   *   *

6. She explains what she does in her leisure time.

How does she spend her time? Mention any **two** things.   **(2)**

*   *   *   *   *

7. She talks about her experiences in school.

What comments does she make about Scottish pupils? Mention any **two** things.   **(2)**

*   *   *   *   *

Marks

8. She compares schools in France with schools in Scotland.

   Why does she prefer the Scottish school system?   Mention any **three** things. **(3)**

   * * * * *

9. She is asked if she misses France.

   Why does she miss French meal times? Mention **two** things. **(2)**

   * * * * *

10. She tells us what she will do next.

    (*a*) What does she plan to do when she returns to France? **(1)**

    (*b*) What does she consider to be important in life? Mention **one** thing. **(1)**

    * * * * *

    Total (25)

[END OF QUESTION PAPER]

[BLANK PAGE]

C

1001/111

SCOTTISH CERTIFICATE OF EDUCATION 1999	WEDNESDAY, 19 MAY 2.55 PM – 3.55 PM	FRENCH STANDARD GRADE Credit Level (Optional Paper) Writing

©

Some young French people talk about their experience of work so far and their future plans.

J'aide mes parents chez moi. Après le dîner, je fais la vaisselle, et je fais parfois la cuisine et le ménage. De temps en temps, je vais chez ma voisine, qui est malade. Je lui fais ses courses.

Blandine, 14 ans

Samedi après-midi, je vais travailler au café du coin pour me faire de l'argent de poche. Je suis serveuse. J'aime cela car je rencontre beaucoup de personnes.

Céline, 16 ans

Plus tard, j'espère être vétérinaire. C'est un métier très bien payé. Je sais que c'est une profession très difficile et que je devrai avoir de très bonnes notes. Mais je suis fort en biologie et j'aime bien les animaux. Je crois que j'y réussirai.

Christophe, 16 ans

Mes parents ne veulent pas que je travaille. Ils pensent que je devrais mieux faire mes devoirs pour avoir de bonnes notes au collège.

Nathalie, 15 ans

Je trouve que c'est important de gagner de l'argent quand on est jeune. J'ai besoin d'argent de poche pour m'acheter des vêtements ou des CD et pour être plus indépendant de mes parents.

Julien, 15 ans

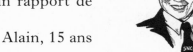

Au mois d'octobre, j'ai fait un stage pendant trois jours à la gare. J'étais au guichet et j'ai vendu des billets aux voyageurs. C'était chouette. Quand je suis revenu au collège, j'ai écrit un rapport de stage.

Alain, 15 ans

Now that you have read what these young people say, write about your own experiences and views.

Here are some questions you may wish to consider. You do not have to use all of them, and you are free to include other relevant ideas.

- Do you help your parents or your neighbours around the house?
- Do you get paid for doing this?
- Do you have a part-time job?
- Should young people work while still at school?
- Is work experience a good idea?
- Is it important to you to be able to earn money of your own?
- What do you do with the money you get?
- What would you like to do after you leave school?

Write about 200 words in **French**.

You may use a French dictionary.

[END OF QUESTION PAPER]

[BLANK PAGE]

1000/403

NATIONAL
QUALIFICATIONS
2000

FRIDAY, 19 MAY
10.25 AM – 11.25 AM

FRENCH
STANDARD GRADE
Credit Level
Reading

Instructions to the Candidate

When you are told to do so, open your paper and write your answers **in English** in the **separate** answer book provided.

You may use a French dictionary.

Marks

1. In a magazine you read an article about the town of Dreux.

À minuit, au lit!

À minuit, on doit rentrer se coucher! C'est ce qu'a décidé Gérard Hamel, le maire de Dreux, pour les enfants de moins de douze ans.

Pendant tout l'été, les moins de douze ans n'ont pas le droit d'être dans la rue, entre minuit et six heures du matin, s'ils ne sont pas accompagnés d'un adulte. C'est pour protéger les jeunes enfants de tous les dangers de la rue, la nuit, explique le maire. Mais il ne veut pas arrêter là. A l'automne, il voudrait priver les parents de leurs *aides sociales s'ils ne surveillent pas leurs enfants.

Dreux est une ville qui est très touchée par le chômage. On connaît des problèmes comme les vols et les agressions. Mais interdire aux plus jeunes d'être dans la rue après minuit, est-ce que cela sera une solution? Pourquoi ne pas donner à tous les habitants de Dreux l'espoir du bonheur et du travail?

*aides sociales—social security payments.

(a) The mayor of Dreux has decided to introduce a curfew for children. Give any **three** details of this scheme.   3

(b) Why has he decided to take this action?   1

(c) How does he intend to penalise parents who do not supervise their children?   1

(d) Mention any **two** social problems which exist in Dreux.   2

(e) The author suggests another solution to the problems of Dreux. What does she suggest?   1

Marks

2. You then read an article about Brazil.

Grande manifestation

Jeudi neuf octobre, à Brasilia, la capitale du Brésil, mille enfants ont manifesté dans les rues. Ils demandent l'interdiction du travail aux enfants de moins de seize ans. Ils veulent avoir le droit d'aller à l'école.

Le Brésil est un pays avec beaucoup de richesses dans son sol, comme le pétrole ou le charbon, mais il n'y a qu'un petit groupe de personnes qui sont très riches. La plupart des Brésiliens sont très pauvres. Ils vivent avec moins de quatre cents francs par mois. Cette misère touche aussi les enfants. Beaucoup d'enfants sont obligés de travailler pour aider leur famille. Aujourd'hui, il y a 3,8 millions d'enfants âgés de cinq à quatorze ans qui travaillent au Brésil. Plus de la moitié de ces enfants travaillent dans des plantations de canne à sucre. D'autres travaillent dans des mines d'argent ou des usines.

Parfois, les enfants sont même abandonnés et ils doivent se débrouiller seuls. C'est ainsi que des milliers d'enfants vendent de la drogue pour pouvoir survivre.

Cependant, le travail des enfants de moins de quatorze ans est déjà interdit par la loi au Brésil. En Norvège, il y aura une conférence internationale. On parlera de la vie des enfants dans le monde et on encouragera les pays à tout faire pour protéger les enfants comme ceux du Brésil.

(*a*) What event took place in Brasilia on 9th October? **1**

(*b*) Why did this event take place? Give **two** reasons. **2**

(*c*) What are we told about the extent of poverty in Brazil today? Mention any **two** things. **2**

(*d*) Mention any **two** types of work done by children. **2**

(*e*) What do thousands of children have to do in order to survive? **1**

(*f*) What will happen at the international conference in Norway? **2**

[Turn over

Marks

3.   An unusual article about garden gnomes catches your eye.

Les voleurs de nains vont être jugés

Une partie des nains retrouvés par les gendarmes.   *(AFP)*

Récemment, des nains de jardin ont disparu mystérieusement des pelouses dans beaucoup de régions de France. Quatre voleurs ont été arrêtés.

Le FLNJ (Front de Libération des Nains de Jardin) existe depuis quelques mois. Ses membres font des farces bizarres. Ils volent des nains qui décorent les pelouses, puis ils les mettent dans les bois ou les forêts. Ils pensent que les nains sont beaucoup plus heureux dans la nature que dans les jardins! Voilà pourquoi des groupes de nains sont trouvés de temps en temps en forêt. La police les rend souvent à leurs propriétaires.

(*a*)   What has been happening recently to garden gnomes in France?   **1**

(*b*)   What exactly do members of the FLNJ do with the garden gnomes?   **1**

(*c*)   Why do they do this?   **1**

Marks

4. The article continues.

> La semaine dernière, la police a arrêté les voleurs de nains à Béthune dans le nord de la France. Ces voleurs, Sébastien, Ludovic, Frédéric et Cédric étaient en train de transporter leurs nains volés sur le siège arrière de leur voiture . . . ils n'avaient même pas essayé de les cacher dans le coffre!
>
> Maintenant, ils vont être jugés. C'est un crime assez sérieux parce que certains des nains volés coûtaient plusieurs centaines de francs la pièce. Les voleurs devront probablement payer une grosse amende ou faire de la prison.

(*a*) Why were Sébastien and his friends so easily caught by the police? Mention **two** things. 2

(*b*) Why is their crime considered to be fairly serious? 1

(*c*) What **two** possible punishments could Sébastien and his friends expect? 2

Total (26)

[*END OF QUESTION PAPER*]

[BLANK PAGE]

[BLANK PAGE]

[BLANK PAGE]

C

1000/409

NATIONAL
QUALIFICATIONS
2000

FRIDAY, 19 MAY
1.30 PM – 2.00 PM
(APPROX.)

FRENCH
STANDARD GRADE
Credit Level
Listening Transcript

This paper must not be seen by any candidate.

The material overleaf is provided for use in an emergency only (eg the tape or equipment proving faulty) or where permission has been given in advance by SQA for the material to be read to candidates with special needs. The material must be read exactly as printed.

SCOTTISH
QUALIFICATIONS
AUTHORITY

Transcript—Credit Level

> **Instructions to reader(s):**
>
> For each item, read the English **once,** then read the French **three times**, with an interval of 5 seconds between the readings. On completion of the third reading, pause for the length of time indicated in brackets after each item, to allow the candidates to write their answers.
>
> Where special arrangements have been agreed in advance to allow the reading of the material, those sections marked **(f)** should be read by a female speaker and those marked **(m)** by a male: those sections marked **(t)** should be read by the teacher.

(t) You are staying with your pen friend Michel. His sister and grandparents arrive to celebrate Michel's mother's birthday.

(f)
or
(m)   *Vous logez chez votre correspondant Michel. Sa soeur et ses grands-parents arrivent pour fêter l'anniversaire de la mère de Michel.*

(t) Question number one.

You're a bit nervous about meeting his family for the first time.

What does Michel say to reassure you?

(m)   *Ne t'inquiète pas. Ma soeur Linette est très sympa; mes grands-parents ont visité l'Écosse il y a quelques années, et ils adorent ton pays.*

(40 seconds)

(t) Question number two.

Linette is an air hostess. You ask her about her job.

Why does she like her job? Give any **two** reasons.

(f)   *Je suis hôtesse de l'air depuis quatre ans maintenant, et j'adore ça! Je trouve que c'est un métier passionnant parce qu'on est toujours en contact avec beaucoup de gens, et aussi, ce qui m'attire dans ce métier, eh bien, ce sont les voyages.*

(40 seconds)

(t) Question number three.

She tells you about her duties.

What does she say? Mention any **two** things.

(f)   *Je dois accueillir les passagers à bord de l'avion et les aider avec leurs petits problèmes. En plus, je dois servir les repas pendant le vol.*

(40 seconds)

(t)   Question number four.

She talks about what makes a good air hostess.

What does she say? Mention **three** things.

(f)   Eh bien, à mon avis, une bonne hôtesse de l'air doit avoir beaucoup de patience. Elle doit aussi être toujours élégante, et il faut parler une langue étrangère au minimum.

(40 seconds)

(t)   Question number five.

There are some disadvantages in her job.

What are they? Mention any **three** things.

(f)   Eh bien, quelquefois je trouve les longs voyages très fatigants. En plus, je n'ai pas beaucoup de temps libre parce que je dois travailler trois semaines sur quatre, donc je ne vois pas souvent ma famille et mes amis.

(40 seconds)

(t)   Question number six.

You have brought a tartan rug for Michel's mother's birthday.

What does she say about your present? Mention **two** things.

(f)   Ah, une couverture écossaise! Elle est très belle! Toutes ces jolies couleurs! Elle sera parfaite pour les pique-niques. Merci beaucoup!

(40 seconds)

(t)   Question number seven.

What does Michel suggest you do the next morning?

Mention **three** things.

(m)   Demain matin, je t'emmène à la banque pour changer ton argent en francs français, et puis tu pourrais acheter des cadeaux pour ta famille et tes copains; et tu as des cartes postales que tu voulais mettre à la poste, n'est-ce pas?

(40 seconds)

(t)   Question number eight.

What does he suggest you do after that?

Mention **three** things.

(m)   Et après ça? Il y a tant de possibilités: je pourrais te montrer mon collège, ou on pourrait faire une promenade en vélo à la campagne, ou bien, si tu préfères, on visitera le vieux quartier de la ville. Qu'est-ce que tu voudrais faire, toi?

(40 seconds)

[Turn over for Questions 9 and 10 on *Page four*

(t) Question number nine.

Michel's mother has other ideas.

What does she suggest? Mention **two** things.

(f)   **Pourquoi pas faire du bateau sur le lac et explorer la petite île qui se trouve au milieu?**

(40 seconds)

(t) Question number ten.

Michel talks about the advantages and disadvantages of living in the country.

Mention **two** advantages.

Mention **one** disadvantage.

(m)   **J'adore vivre ici. C'est bien pour les jeunes et il n'y a pas beaucoup de violence. L'air est frais et je me sens libre. Mais après le collège, j'aurai des difficultés à trouver un emploi. Donc, pour avoir un travail, je devrai déménager en ville.**

(40 seconds)

(t) End of test.

Now look over your answers.

[END OF TRANSCRIPT]

C

1000/408

NATIONAL
QUALIFICATIONS
2000

FRIDAY, 19 MAY
1.30 PM – 2.00 PM
(APPROX.)

FRENCH
STANDARD GRADE
Credit Level
Listening

Instructions to the Candidate

When you are told to do so, open your paper.

You will hear a number of short items in French. You will hear each item three times, then you will have time to write your answer.

Write your answers, **in English**, in the **separate** answer book provided.

You may take notes as you are listening to the French, but only in your answer book.

You may **not** use a French dictionary.

You are not allowed to leave the examination room until the end of the test.

SCOTTISH
QUALIFICATIONS
AUTHORITY

©

Marks

You are staying with your pen friend Michel. His sister and grandparents arrive to celebrate Michel's mother's birthday.

Vous logez chez votre correspondant Michel. Sa soeur et ses grands-parents arrivent pour fêter l'anniversaire de la mère de Michel.

1. You're a bit nervous about meeting his family for the first time.

    What does Michel say to reassure you?   2

    *   *   *   *   *

2. Linette is an air hostess. You ask her about her job.

    Why does she like her job? Give any **two** reasons.   2

    *   *   *   *   *

3. She tells you about her duties.

    What does she say? Mention any **two** things.   2

    *   *   *   *   *

4. She talks about what makes a good air hostess. What does she say?

    Mention **three** things.   3

    *   *   *   *   *

5. There are some disadvantages in her job.

    What are they? Mention any **three** things.   3

    *   *   *   *   *

6. You have brought a tartan rug for Michel's mother's birthday.

    What does she say about your present? Mention **two** things.   2

    *   *   *   *   *

7. What does Michel suggest you do the next morning?

    Mention **three** things.   3

    *   *   *   *   *

8. What does he suggest you do after that?

    Mention **three** things.   3

    *   *   *   *   *

Marks

9. Michel's mother has other ideas.

   What does she suggest? Mention **two** things. 2

        *   *   *   *   *

10. Michel talks about the advantages and disadvantages of living in the country.

    (*a*) Mention **two** advantages. 2

    (*b*) Mention **one** disadvantage. 1

        *   *   *   *   *

Total (25)

[END OF QUESTION PAPER]

[BLANK PAGE]

C

1001/411

NATIONAL
QUALIFICATIONS
2000

THURSDAY, 25 MAY
2.55 PM – 3.55 PM

FRENCH
STANDARD GRADE
Credit Level
(Additional)
Writing

SCOTTISH
QUALIFICATIONS
AUTHORITY

Several French teenagers comment on fashion and money.

A mon avis, suivre la mode coûte trop cher. Pour moi, ce qui est plus important, c'est le confort. De temps en temps, il me faut une paire de chaussures de sport pour le football ou peut-être un T-shirt et c'est tout. Cela me suffit.

Romain, 15 ans

Si je ne fais rien de spécial, j'aime mettre quelque chose de confortable comme un jean et un sweatshirt. Par contre, le soir, si je sors à la disco, j'aime me faire beau.

Youenne, 16 ans

Je m'intéresse à la mode. J'essaie d'acheter mes vêtements dans les soldes. Cela me permet d'acheter des vêtements de marque, qui sont de meilleure qualité. Un jour, j'aimerais devenir mannequin.

Céline, 16 ans

C'est moi qui paie mes vêtements. J'ai un petit boulot le weekend et une fois par mois, je vais dans les boutiques. Mais je dépense mon argent en magazines aussi. En ce moment, j'économise pour payer un voyage scolaire aux Etats Unis.

Anne, 16 ans

Je n'ai pas d'emploi mais j'ai toujours de l'argent. Si je veux gagner un peu d'argent, j'aide mes parents à la maison. Par exemple, mes parents me donnent une certaine somme si je garde ma petite soeur le soir ou si je passe l'aspirateur le weekend.

Aurélie, 15 ans

Now that you have read what these people say about fashion and money, give your own opinions.

Here are some questions you may wish to consider. You do not have to use all of them, and you are free to include other relevant ideas of your own.

- Is fashion important in your opinion?

- What sorts of clothes do you wear for different occasions?

- Where do you shop for your clothes and who pays?

- Do you shop alone or with friends or family?

- What else do you spend your money on?

- How do you get your money?

Write about 200 words in **French**.

You may use a French dictionary.

[END OF QUESTION PAPER]

[BLANK PAGE]

C

1000/403

NATIONAL
QUALIFICATIONS
2001

FRIDAY, 18 MAY
10.25 AM – 11.25 AM

FRENCH
STANDARD GRADE
Credit Level
Reading

Instructions to the Candidate

When you are told to do so, open your paper and write your answers **in English** in the **separate** answer book provided.

You may use a French dictionary.

SCOTTISH
QUALIFICATIONS
AUTHORITY

©

Marks

1. While reading through a newspaper for young people, you find an article on pocket money. It explains why young people should have pocket money.

"J'aimerais avoir plus d'argent . . .
  Qu'est-ce que je peux faire, Eric?"

Ça, c'est la question que Julien a posée à Eric.

Voici la réponse qu'Eric lui a donnée:

"Comme tu es trop jeune pour travailler, c'est sûr que tu as besoin d'argent de poche. Sinon, tu devrais rester enfermé dans ta chambre et donc tu ne pourrais pas sortir avec tes copains.

La plupart des parents donnent à leurs enfants une somme d'argent qui leur permet de gérer leur budget et d'apprendre à être plus indépendants. Vêtements, ciné et musique, voilà les dépenses les plus importantes quand on est adolescent. Et c'est vrai que les achats peuvent très vite éclater ton budget."

(a) Why can Julien not earn his own money?   **1**

(b) Without money, what would life be like for Julien?   **1**

(c) Most parents give their children some pocket money. What does this teach young people to do?   **2**

(d) Why are clothes, cinema and music mentioned?   **1**

Marks

2. In the article, Eric goes on to give tips to young people on how to earn money.

> "Et voici quelques conseils:
>
> Cet argent dont tu as besoin, il faut le gagner. Comment? Il existe un tas de petits boulots qui peuvent te rapporter un peu d'argent: livraison de journaux, emballage de cadeaux, lavage de voitures, arrosage de plantes . . . Cependant, il y a certains petits boulots qui se divisent traditionnellement par genre; par exemple, près de la moitié des filles gardent des enfants pour les voisins alors que les garçons font plutôt des travaux agricoles saisonniers. Mais il faut avoir 14 ans pour faire la plupart des petits boulots.
>
> Alors, en attendant, demande à tes voisins ou à d'autres membres de ta famille s'ils n'ont pas un travail domestique à te donner, par exemple une vieille porte à repeindre. Mais n'oublie pas de leur dire avant de commencer que tout travail mérite un salaire.
>
> Mais attention! Aucune de ces tâches ne doit t'empêcher de faire tes devoirs!!"

(a) What could you do to earn some money? Mention any **two** jobs.   2

(b) What specific task is traditionally popular with teenage girls? And with boys?   2

(c) What restriction is there in doing these part-time jobs in France?   1

(d) If you do something for your family or a friend, what should you tell them before you start?   1

(e) What final word of warning does Eric give you?   1

[Turn over

Marks

3. You read another article discussing the problem of racism in France.

Dire Non au Racisme

Etre raciste, c'est mépriser l'autre parce qu'il est différent de soi. Les personnes racistes ont souvent peur de ceux qui ne sont pas comme elles. Elles croient que "l'Etranger" représente une menace pour leur sécurité et leur emploi, ce qui est faux.

En France, le racisme est puni par la loi. Cependant, nous sommes témoins de propos ou d'attitudes racistes partout dans la société. Ainsi, certains propriétaires préfèrent louer ou vendre leur appartement à un Blanc plutôt qu'à un Noir, par exemple. D'autre part, souvent des gens ne sont pas admis à certains lieux publics à cause de la couleur de leur peau. Et, à l'école, les enfants d'origine étrangère sont parfois exposés aux plaisanteries de leurs camarades pour leur accent ou leur origine.

Une étude récente montre que les jeunes d'origine étrangère ont plus de mal que les autres à trouver du travail, par exemple un jeune sur deux, né de parents algériens, est au chômage. Pourtant les jeunes nés en France de parents français sont seulement un sur dix à être sans emploi.

Ces inégalités de traitement sont punies par la loi française. Mais en réalité, très peu de gens coupables sont punis. Pourquoi? D'abord, les victimes doivent prouver qu'elles ont subi des actes racistes, et puis très peu d'entre elles portent plainte. C'est à nous d'être attentifs à toutes les attitudes racistes. Apporter son témoignage est un acte de solidarité.

(a) What, according to the author, often causes people to be racist? Mention any **one** thing.   **1**

(b) What **three** examples are given of racist behaviour in French society?   **3**

(c) A recent study looked at the employment prospects for young people in France. What were the findings of this study? Mention any **two** things.   **2**

(d) Discrimination is punishable by law. Why are so few people convicted of racial discrimination? Mention **two** things.   **2**

(e) What does the author challenge us to do? Mention any **one** thing.   **1**

Marks

4. This article considers the growth in popularity of working from home.

Travailler à la maison

Beaucoup de gens rêvent de travailler chez eux au lieu d'avoir à se rendre au bureau tous les jours. Environ trois cent mille Français ont déjà adopté le 'télétravail', c'est-à-dire le travail à distance. Ce sont par exemple des traducteurs, des secrétaires, des architectes, des informaticiens.

Le télétravail intéresse de nombreuses entreprises qui n'ont plus à louer ou à acheter un bureau pour leurs employés. Il séduit les travailleurs qui ne perdent plus leur temps dans les transports et peuvent choisir librement leur temps de travail.

En revanche, cette liberté entraîne un certain isolement mais aussi une responsabilité et une discipline supplémentaires. Il n'est pas toujours facile de travailler chez soi quand il fait beau ou quand les enfants jouent à côté.

(*a*) This article talks about the advantages of working from home.

   (i) Mention **one** advantage for employers.　　　　　　　**1**

   (ii) Mention **two** advantages for workers.　　　　　　　**2**

(*b*) It also talks of the disadvantages for workers. Mention any **two**.　　**2**

Total (26)

[END OF QUESTION PAPER]

[BLANK PAGE]

[BLANK PAGE]

[BLANK PAGE]

C

1000/409

NATIONAL QUALIFICATIONS 2001	FRIDAY, 18 MAY 1.30 PM – 2.00 PM (APPROX.)	**FRENCH STANDARD GRADE** Credit Level Listening Transcript

This paper must not be seen by any candidate.

The material overleaf is provided for use in an emergency only (eg the tape or equipment proving faulty) or where permission has been given in advance by SQA for the material to be read to candidates with special needs. The material must be read exactly as printed.

SCOTTISH QUALIFICATIONS AUTHORITY

©

Transcript—Credit Level

> **Instructions to reader(s):**
>
> For each item, read the English **once,** then read the French **three times**, with an interval of 5 seconds between the readings. On completion of the third reading, pause for the length of time indicated in brackets after each item, to allow the candidates to write their answers.
>
> Where special arrangements have been agreed in advance to allow the reading of the material, those sections marked **(f)** should be read by a female speaker and those marked **(m)** by a male: those sections marked **(t)** should be read by the teacher.

(t) You and your pen friend are listening to a programme for young people on French radio. A film director is talking about one of her recent films.

(f)　　　　**Pendant ton séjour en France, tu écoutes une émission à la radio avec ton correspondant**
or　　　　**français. Une réalisatrice parle d'un de ses films.**
(m)

(t) **Question number one.**

Where did the inspiration come from to make the film?

Which human qualities are depicted in the film? Mention any **two**.

(f)　　　　**Le film est inspiré d'un magnifique poème chinois. C'est une histoire sur le courage,**
　　　　　　l'amitié, la vérité et le respect des traditions chinoises.

(40 seconds)

(t) **Question number two.**

She goes on to explain the appearance in the story of the dragon.

What does she say? Mention any **two** things.

(f)　　　　**Les dragons font partie de l'histoire de la Chine. Dans les légendes de la Chine, il y a**
　　　　　　beaucoup d'animaux et le dragon occupe la première place. C'est le symbole de la force
　　　　　　masculine.

(40 seconds)

(t) **Question number three.**

After the interview, the presenter reminds you that Father's Day is coming up.

Why, according to the presenter, should you take this opportunity to say "thank you" to your dad? Mention any **three** things.

(f)　　　　**Dimanche prochain, c'est la Fête des Pères. C'est vrai qu'on ne le voit pas souvent. Mais**
or　　　　**ça, c'est parce qu'il travaille. Quand il est là, il s'occupe bien de nous. Il nous aide pour**
(m)　　　　**les devoirs, il écoute nos problèmes et puis, le weekend, il nous donne l'argent nécessaire**
　　　　　　pour nos sorties. Eh bien, profitez de la Fête des Pères pour lui dire un grand merci pour
　　　　　　tout.

(40 seconds)

(t) Question number four.

There is a break for the news. One news item tells of the havoc wreaked by the monsoon in Asia.

What have been the effects of the monsoon? Mention any **four** things.

(f)
or
(m)
> **En Asie, en ce moment, c'est la période de la mousson. A cause des pluies torrentielles et des vents très forts, les rues sont transformées en rivières et il y a des maisons et des ponts détruits. On compte déjà près de mille morts. Beaucoup de gens ont perdu leur maison. Ils manquent d'eau potable et de nourriture. Malheureusement, la mousson risque de durer encore quelques semaines.**

(40 seconds)

(t) After the break Philippe Fragione, singer with a famous rap group, talks about his life.

Question number five.

He mentions his childhood and his teenage years.

As a child what did he hope to be? Mention any **one** thing.

What was he like as a teenager? Mention any **one** thing.

(m)
> **Quand j'étais petit, je voulais devenir archéologue, ou sportif professionnel—dans n'importe quel sport—rugby, tennis, foot. Comme adolescent, j'étais assez timide. Je passais beaucoup de temps dans ma chambre.**

(40 seconds)

(t) Question number six.

Why does he not go out a lot?

What does he do instead?

(m)
> **On me fait souvent le reproche "tu ne sors jamais". Et bien, les sorties, ça ne m'intéresse pas du tout et puis je ne bois pas. Je préfère rester chez moi à composer des chansons ou à lire des livres historiques.**

(40 seconds)

(t) Question number seven.

Philippe converted to Islam ten years ago.

What made him decide to become a Muslim? Mention any **two** things.

(m)
> **J'ai décidé de me convertir à l'Islam il y a 10 ans. La plupart de mes copains étaient d'origine arabe et donc j'ai commencé à lire le Coran. C'est le côté spirituel de l'Islam que je trouve intéressant.**

(40 seconds)

[Turn over for Question 8 on *Page four*

(t) Question number eight.

What was life like for him between 1993 and 1997?

What is it like now? Mention any **three** things.

(m)   **Je n'oublie jamais les quatre années entre 1993 et 1997 quand je n'avais pas de travail et que je vivais dans la rue. Mais aujourd'hui, je gagne de l'argent, j'ai une femme, un fils et une vie équilibrée. Je mange et je dors à des heures précises. J'ai de la chance.**

(40 seconds)

(t) End of test.

Now look over your answers.

[END OF TRANSCRIPT]

1000/408

NATIONAL
QUALIFICATIONS
2001

FRIDAY, 18 MAY
1.30 PM – 2.00 PM
(APPROX.)

FRENCH
STANDARD GRADE
Credit Level
Listening

Instructions to the Candidate

When you are told to do so, open your paper.

You will hear a number of short items in French. You will hear each item three times, then you will have time to write your answer.

Write your answers, **in English**, in the **separate** answer book provided.

You may take notes as you are listening to the French, but only in your answer book.

You may **not** use a French dictionary.

You are not allowed to leave the examination room until the end of the test.

Marks

You and your pen friend are listening to a programme for young people on French radio. A film director is talking about one of her recent films.

Pendant ton séjour en France, tu écoutes une émission à la radio avec ton correspondant français. Une réalisatrice parle d'un de ses films.

1.   (a) Where did the inspiration come from to make the film?   1

    (b) Which human qualities are depicted in the film? Mention any **two**.   2

                  *   *   *   *   *

2.   She goes on to explain the appearance in the story of the dragon.

    What does she say? Mention any **two** things.   2

                  *   *   *   *   *

3.   After the interview, the presenter reminds you that Father's Day is coming up.

    Why, according to the presenter, should you take this opportunity to say "thank you" to your dad? Mention any **three** things.   3

                  *   *   *   *   *

4.   There is a break for the news. One news item tells of the havoc wreaked by the monsoon in Asia.

    What have been the effects of the monsoon? Mention any **four** things.   4

                  *   *   *   *   *

After the break Philippe Fragione, singer with a famous rap group, talks about his life.

5.   He mentions his childhood and his teenage years.

    (a) As a child what did he hope to be? Mention any **one** thing.   1

    (b) What was he like as a teenager? Mention any **one** thing.   1

                  *   *   *   *   *

6.   (a) Why does he not go out a lot?   2

    (b) What does he do instead?   2

                  *   *   *   *   *

Marks

7. Philippe converted to Islam ten years ago.

   What made him decide to become a Muslim? Mention any **two** things. 2

   *   *   *   *   *

8. (*a*) What was life like for him between 1993 and 1997? 2

   (*b*) What is it like now? Mention any **three** things. 3

   *   *   *   *   *

Total (25)

[*END OF QUESTION PAPER*]

[BLANK PAGE]

C

1001/411

NATIONAL
QUALIFICATIONS
2001

THURSDAY, 24 MAY
2.55 PM – 3.55 PM

FRENCH
STANDARD GRADE
Credit Level
(Additional)
Writing

Some French teenagers talk about their schools. They say what they like and dislike.

Ce que j'aime, c'est qu'on n'a pas cours le mercredi. Des fois, je fais la grasse matinée jusqu'à onze heures et puis je sors en ville avec mes amis.

Vincent, 16 ans

C'est dommage qu'il n'y ait pas d'uniforme scolaire à mon collège. Le matin, j'ai toujours du mal à décider quels vêtements je veux porter et par conséquent j'arrive souvent en retard.

Emilie, 14 ans

A mon avis, on commence trop tôt le matin. J'ai une demi-heure de route en car pour aller au collège. Je dois me lever à six heures et quart. Le soir, je suis crevé.

Nicolas, 15 ans

Je vais à un très bon collège. Les professeurs semblent tous aimer leur travail, le bâtiment est ultramoderne et j'ai beaucoup de copines intimes. Je sais que j'ai de la chance.

Pauline, 15 ans

Si je pouvais changer une chose, ce serait les matières que je dois faire. Je ne comprends pas pourquoi je suis obligé d'étudier le latin quand j'ai l'intention de devenir ingénieur.

Antoine, 16 ans

J'aimerais aller à un collège où tout le monde se tutoie, où personne ne s'ennuie jamais. J'aimerais un collège moins autoritaire et plus démocratique où les élèves ont le droit de participer à la prise des décisions.

Nadine, 15 ans

Now that you have read what these young people say, write about your own school.

Here are some questions you may wish to consider. You do not have to use all of them, and you are free to include other relevant ideas of your own.

- What is your school like?

- What rules does your school have?

- What do you like about your school?

- What do you dislike about your school?

- What facilities would you like to have in your school?

- What rights would you like to have?

- What would be your ideal school?

Write about 200 words in **French**.

You may use a French dictionary.

[END OF QUESTION PAPER]

[BLANK PAGE]

French Credit Level— Reading 2000

1. (a) it's for the summer

    for under twelves/children up to 12

    it operates from <u>midnight</u> (till six in the morning)/children have to be in by midnight/in bed by midnight

    children must be accompanied by an adult

    (3 from 4)

    (b) to keep children out of trouble

    to protect young people/ children/them/youths

    it's dangerous <u>at night</u>/<u>on the street(s)</u>

    (1 from 2)

    (c) by withdrawing/freezing/ stopping/cutting off/depriving financial support/ social security payment(s)

    (d) (high) unemployment

    theft/robbery/stealing/thieving

    violence/attacks/muggings/ fights/acts of aggression/ assaults

    (2 from 3)

    (e) giving the people of Dreux <u>the hope/prospect/opportunity/ chance of</u> happiness/work

2. (a) demonstration/march/protest <u>by</u> (1000) <u>children</u>/children took to the streets

    (b) they want (a law) to ban children <u>under 16</u> from working

    they want (to be allowed) to go to school/they want to be educated/should go/must go to school

    (c) 3·8 million children/millions of children between 5 and 14 work/(lots of) children work to help their family

    the poor in Brazil/<u>most</u> Brazilians live on/have/earn/ work for <u>less than</u> 400 francs <u>a month</u>

    there is only a small group of rich people/<u>most</u> Brazilians are poor

    (2 from 3)

    (d) work on sugar plantations/ fields/work with sugar cane/ planting sugar cane

    in silver mines

    in factories/factory work

    (2 from 3)

    (e) sell drugs/deal drugs

    (f) talk about (the life of) children <u>throughout the world</u>

    encourage countries to (do what they can to) protect children

3. (a) disappearing/being stolen/going missing

    (b) put them in woods/forests

French Credit Level— Reading 2000

    (c) (think) they'll be (much) <u>happier</u> (there) (than in a garden)

4. (a) carrying gnomes in the back of the car/on (back) seat of car/in full view in the car

          didn't (even) try to hide them (in boot) (in trunk)

    (b) <u>some of</u>/<u>certain</u> gnomes have a high value/are expensive/worth several hundred/cost hundreds of francs/per piece/a piece/each

    (c) (pay) a large/big/hefty/fat fine (go to) prison

French Credit Level— Listening 2000

1. don't worry

      sister (very) nice/pleasant/ friendly

      grandparents like Scotland/ grandparents have been to Scotland and loved it

      (2 from 3)

2. it's exciting/exhilarating/thrilling

      meet/have contact with (lots of) people/passengers/talking with the passengers/gets to be in among lots of people

      the travel/travelling/the journey(s)/ travel around the world

      (2 from 3)

3. <u>welcomes</u>/<u>greets</u> passengers (on board)

    helps (them) with (little) <u>problem</u>(s)/listens to <u>problem</u>(s) and helps them/sorts out <u>problem</u>(s)/deals with <u>problem</u>(s)/solves <u>problem</u>(s)

    serves <u>meals</u>/serves <u>food</u>

    (2 from 3)

4. patience

    (always) elegant/chic/classy/smart/ smartly dressed/sophisticated

    speak (minimum/at least) a/one (foreign) language/another language/two languages/a different language/other languages/speak one language other than French

5. (long) journeys/flights/travel are <u>tiring</u>/long distances

    not much time to relax/not much free time/she gets limited free time

    works 3 weeks out of 4/3 weeks in a month/works for 3 weeks at a time/solid/ without a break/gets one week off in 4

    doesn't see much of family/friends misses her family/friends/doesn't get to see her family/friends (much)/she's away from her family a lot

    (3 from 4)

6. <u>colour(s)</u> are lovely/nice/pretty/it's beautiful/she likes/loves the colours

    ideal/perfect/good for picnics/she can use it for a picnic

7. (ex)change money (at the bank) (into French francs)/exchange your Scottish/English money

    buy presents/gifts <u>for family/ parents/friends</u>

    send postcard<u>s</u>/post card<u>s</u>

French Credit Level— Listening 2000

8. show (round) school/(go and) see the school/visit the school/have a look round the school/tour the school

go for a bike run <u>in the country/ countryside</u>/go for a cycle <u>in the country</u>

visit the old town/old area(s)/old quarter(s)/bit(s) <u>of the town</u>

9. go boating/sailing/get a boat/go <u>on</u> the lake/go on a boat ride/trip

<u>explore</u> island (in the middle of the lake)

10. (a) good for young people/the young

not much violence

fresh air/clean air/no pollution

feel free/more freedom/have lots of freedom

(2 from 4)

(b) no work/hard to get work/can't get work/no jobs/not many jobs/there are more jobs in town/(have to) move/go to town for work/more jobs in town

French Credit Level— Reading 2001

1. (a) too young (to work)/not old enough

(b) (would have to) stay in <u>his room</u>/trapped/stuck/shut in <u>his room</u>

could never/couldn't see/ wouldn't come/go/come out with <u>friend(s)</u>

(1 from 2)

(c) manage/control/handle/look after their budget/money

live on/manage on a budget/ budget (their money)

be <u>more</u> independent

(d) they are what (most) young folk/they/children/adolescents spend (most of) their money on/buy

these things take a lot of their money

2. (a) deliver papers/paper-boy/-girl

wrap up presents/packaging gifts

wash/clean car(s)

water plants

(2 from 4)

(b) girls—babysitting/looking after/watching (neighbours') children

boys—(seasonal) farm/ agricultural work/work in the fields/farming/farmer

(c) must be (over/at least) 14

(d) you want to/expect to/deserve to/should be paid/all jobs require a salary/wage

(e) don't forget to do/don't let the jobs stop you from doing your homework/studying/school work

make sure you do your homework/homework comes first/before work

homework is more important

don't let job interfere with homework

French Credit Level— Reading 2001

3. (*a*) fear/afraid/frightened of others' difference(s)
they think foreigners are a threat/menace to their safety/job(s)/security
(1 from 2)

(*b*) owners prefer (more often) to sell/rent their flats/houses/accommodation to Whites/Whites get flats before Blacks

people are refused entry (to public places) because of (skin) <u>colour</u>

black people are refused entry

foreign children can be teased/picked on/bullied/get called names/get jokes made about them by classmates/friends (at school) (because of accent/origin/colour)

(*c*) more foreigners are unemployed
(young) foreigners/coloured people have more difficulty in finding work/ more (young) people with French parents have jobs than people with Algerian parents

French people are more likely to get jobs (than foreigners/other races)

1 in 2 people whose parents are Algerian are (un)employed

1 in 10 people/children whose parents are French are unemployed
(2 from 3)

(*d*) victims must be able to prove it/(racial abuse/racist acts/incidents)/discrimination
victims can't/don't prove (racial abuse/racist acts/incidents)
it's hard to prove it/their case

very few people complain/speak out

people/they/victims keep quiet/never/don't complain/report incidents

(*e*) Watch out for/pay attention to/be vigilant about/don't ignore any racist attitudes/racism
(Show solidarity by)/acting as/being a witness/coming forward/speaking up/testifying (against racists)/give evidence
(1 from 2)

4. (*a*) (i) don't need to rent/buy/have/provide office/premises/workplace (for their employees)

(ii) don't waste time travelling/don't have to travel/no travelling involved/save time travelling/don't need transport
can choose times to work/can work when you want to/at your leisure

French Credit Level—Reading 2001

(b) can isolate you/make you lonely/you feel cut off

you'd always be on your own

gives you extra/more/added/further responsibility/you have to be more responsible/requires extra discipline

not easy to work when it's nice (weather)/children are around/playing near

children at home may distract you

(2 from 3)

French Credit Level—Listening 2001

1. (a) (magnificent/Chinese) poem/China/China poem

   (b) courage/bravery

   friendship

   truth/honesty/verity

   respect for (Chinese) tradition(s)

   (2 from 4)

2. it is/they are part of/in Chinese history/legend

   the dragon is the most important animal/occupies first place (in Chinese legends/history)

   it represents/is the symbol of masculine strength/power/force

   (2 from 3)

3. you don't see him often/he works (a lot/hard/to provide for us)/he earns money for you

   he looks after us/takes care of us/attends to us/spends time with us

   he helps us with (home) work/studies

   he listens to our problems

   he gives us (pocket) money (for going out/at the weekend/every week)/when we need it

   (3 from 5)

4. there is torrential rain

   high/strong winds

   road(s)/street(s) are like rivers/flooded

   bridges destroyed

   (roughly/nearly a) thousand dead/deaths

   (lots of) people lost their homes/houses/homeless/houses destroyed/ruined/wrecked

   houses blown/swept/washed away

   shortage/not enough/lack of/hardly any/no drinking water/food

   (4 from 7)

5. (a) archaeologist

   professional sportsman/sports professional/athlete/star/person/player/tennis player/football player/rugby player

   (1 from 2)

   (b) (quite) shy/timid/quiet

   spends/passes lots of time in his room/on his own/was a loner/stayed in his room

   (1 from 2)

French Credit Level— Listening 2001

6. (a) he's not interested in/does not like it/(going out)/prefers staying in/would rather stay in
   he doesn't drink

   (b) makes up/composes/writes <u>songs</u>
   reads history/historic(al) books/ books about history/studies history/reads about history

7. (most of/all) his friend<u>s</u> were/are Arab
   he started reading/wanted to read the Koran/Muslim bible
   he liked/was interested in the spiritual/religious <u>aspect</u>/<u>side</u>/ <u>nature</u>/<u>ways</u>/<u>part</u>/<u>element</u>
   (2 from 3)

8. (a) he had no job/work/didn't work/never worked
   he lived in/on the streets/was homeless/lived rough

   (b) he earns/has (more) sufficient/ plenty money/has a job
   he is married/has a wife/woman
   he has a son/child/family
   he leads/has a balanced/stable life
   he eats/sleeps at set/regular/ exact/precise/proper times
   (3 from 5)

French Credit Level— Writing 2000 and 2001

Writing – Summary GRC

At both Levels candidates were permitted to use a dictionary.

  General Level (grades 4, 3)

  The candidate communicated with some success in writing simple messages.

  Credit Level (grades 2, 1)

  The candidate communicated information and personal opinions with clarity, showing some facility in the use of the language.

Descriptions of Grades

These describe performances within Levels.

Grade 4   The candidate met the criteria for General Level, demonstrating a satisfactory overall standard of performance.

Grade 3   The candidate met the criteria for General Level, demonstrating a high overall standard of performance.

Grade 2   The candidate met the criteria for Credit Level, demonstrating a satisfactory overall standard of performance.

Grade 1   The candidate met the criteria for Credit Level, demonstrating a high overall standard of performance.

French Credit Level— Writing 2000 and 2001

Writing – Extended GRC

At both Levels candidates are permitted to use a dictionary.

General Level (grades 4, 3)

The candidate can communicate with some success although there are many errors and inaccuracies in what he/she has written.

His/Her range of vocabulary and structures allows him/her to give and ask for straightforward information with some elaboration of basic statements.

Credit Level (grades 2, 1)

The candidate has no difficulty in making himself/herself understood, although there may be some errors and inaccuracies in what he/she has written.

His/Her range of vocabulary and structures allows him/her to give straightforward information and express personal opinions with clarity and in an ordered fashion. His/Her language flows freely and naturally, and shows some variety in sentence construction.